deeplove

GUIDE
FOR COUPLES

Drs. Les & Leslie Parrott

Before you begin this study, you will need to take the Deep Love Assessment at Outreach.DeepLoveAssessment.com.

This guide will only make sense when it accompanies your own ten-page report—personalized for just the two of you.

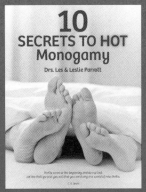

Deep Love is a unique and powerful online assessment that takes just fifteen minutes to complete. It generates a personalized ten-page report for couples (whether dating, engaged, or married for decades). The personalized Deep Love Report can be explored in small groups, classes, or simply as a couple. It's for couples who want to move from bad to better as well as those moving from good to great and beyond.

Each of the four sections of the report—Personality, Communication, Conflict, and Adaptability—are essential to deepening the relationship with lasting, positive results.

PERSONALITY

When it comes to personalities, there's no right or perfect combination. The key is appreciating your differences.

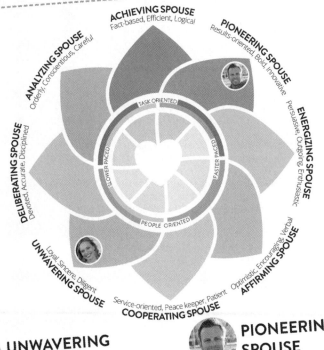

ACHIEVING SPOUSE
Fact-based, Efficient, Logical

ANALYZING SPOUSE
Orderly, Conscientious, Careful

PIONEERING SPOUSE
Results-oriented, Bold, Innovative

DELIBERATING SPOUSE
Devoted, Accurate, Disciplined

ENERGIZING SPOUSE
Persuasive, Outgoing, Enthusiastic

TASK ORIENTED

SLOWER PACED

FASTER PACED

PEOPLE ORIENTED

UNWAVERING SPOUSE
Loyal, Sincere, Diligent

AFFIRMING SPOUSE
Optimistic, Encouraging, Verbal

COOPERATING SPOUSE
Service-oriented, Peace keeper, Patient

UNWAVERING SPOUSE

You may demonstrate positive possessiveness by developing strong attachments; however, you will not be overly involved as some others tend to do. You are a good friend and are always willing to help those you consider to be your friends. You also show strong ties, and will be uncomfortable when separated from your friends for an extended period. You

PIONEERING SPOUSE

You may be restless and may display anxiety by failing to sit quietly through any situation in which you have no opportunity for involvement. You make fast decisions and quickly respond to new ideas and activities. You may encourage your spouse to participate as well. You show a high activity level in all that you do. The fast pace by which you accomplish tasks and the variety of interests you show ... activity level. Few dull moments

OUTRE*CH®

Deep Love Guide
© 2016 by Outreach, Inc.

Published by Outreach, Inc., Colorado Springs, CO 80919
www.Outreach.com

ISBN: 9781635100426
Cover Design by Tim Downs
Interior Design by Alexia Garaventa

Printed in the United States of America

CONTENTS

GETTING THE MOST FROM YOUR DEEP LOVE REPORT

Have you ever heard of the KISS principle? It's an acronym coined by the US Navy in the 1960s. It stands for "Keep It Simple and Straightforward."

That's exactly what we're going to do for you in this guide to your Deep Love Report. We assume you've already taken the Deep Love Assessment (or will shortly). You've each answered the items that have generated your personalized ten-page Deep Love Report, and we're eager to walk you through it. Keep it handy.

But back to the KISS principle. Building a healthy and loving relationship does not have to be complicated. Of course, that doesn't mean it's simple, either. In fact, when you join two unique personalities—each with their own set of feelings, desires, and wills—and put them into the grind of daily life with the intention to maintain the ideal of love, it gets complicated. But that's exactly why we developed the Deep Love Assessment. We're doing the complicated work for you in order to deliver a straightforward experience with a big payoff.

This guide has four primary sessions, each corresponding to a section of your Deep Love Report:

1. **Personality**—because it's the best way to enhance empathy
2. **Communication**—because it's the lifeblood of love
3. **Conflict**—because every couple has friction
4. **Adaptability**—because even good marriages bump into bad things

Each of these sections is essential to deepening your relationship. They get right to the point and help you see what matters most. We're going to give you practical exercises for each one and then guide you through a series of conversations with each other that are sure to bring you closer together.

Many couples enjoy processing their Deep Love Report in a small group with other couples. Deep Love works extremely well in groups. For this reason, you'll find a portion of each section with specific directions for groups.

The final page of your Deep Love Report helps the two of you devise a next-step plan for taking your experience to an even deeper level.

TIPS FOR MAXIMIZING YOUR DEEP LOVE EXPERIENCE

Here are a few time-tested recommendations:

- Purposefully set aside time to review your report together. Don't do it on the run. You may want to do this on a date night after you've shared a meal and you're in a quiet place.

- Most couples find it helpful to schedule four "dates" on the calendar to reserve time for processing the report together.

- You'll each want something to write with for taking a few notes.

- Turn off all distractions (yup, that means your phones).

- Each session is designed to take about an hour—but that all depends upon the length of your conversations.

- Don't get hung up on getting through every piece of your session. You can always come back to what you didn't get to at a later time.

- Only do a session when both of you can be fully present.

- Commit to keeping the conversations positive. Don't use information from your report to criticize each other. That defeats the entire purpose.

- Review your Deep Love Report from time to time over the next few months—it will help you continually put what you learn into practice.

If you commit to going through each of these sections with intention, if you come to this with an open heart and an eagerness to learn, you are sure to find a way to enjoy a love that grows deeper and deeper along the way.

After all, none of us is interested in a shallow relationship, right? We don't want to hover around the surface. We want to sink the roots of our relationship deep into love. We want to enjoy deeper connection and understanding. Deeper conversations and bonding. Deeper intimacy and passion. And that's exactly what Deep Love can do for you.

Drs. Les & Leslie Parrott
Founders of the Deep Love Assessment

SESSION ONE

PERSONALITY

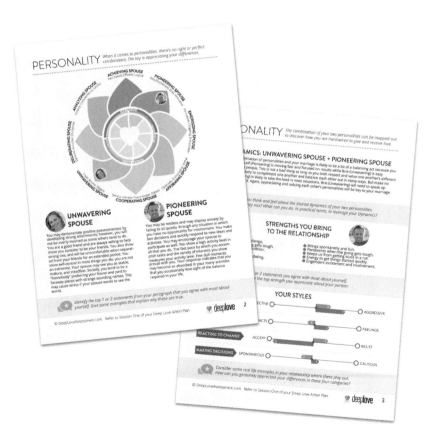

HOW UNDERSTANDING YOUR PERSONALITIES LEADS TO DEEP LOVE

One of the most important ways for deepening your connection with your partner is to understand yourselves and each other—deep down in the DNA of your personalities. Why? Because the more awareness and insight you have about how each of you is made, the more empathy you have for one another. And empathy is at the heart of love. More than any other single deficiency, a lack of mutual empathy prevents couples from enjoying deep love. If there is any great secret to success in love found in the top 10 percent of deeply fulfilled and loving couples, it's the capacity to put themselves in each other's shoes. This session will show the two of you how to do that like never before.

1 EXERCISE
YOU'RE A ONE-OF-A-KIND COUPLE

Your relationship is unique. There's never been a couple like you before—and there never will be again. The combination of your two unique personalities makes for a one-of-a-kind partnership. So, to get your wheels turning right from the outset, consider what makes your relationship distinctive. Below is a diagram representing you and your partner. On the lines provided, write three special qualities that are particularly noticeable in each of your personalities.

HIS TRAITS   **HER TRAITS**

_____   _____

_____   _____

_____   _____

Now, as you consider the six qualities you've noted above, each of you can draw a line from one of your own qualities to one of the qualities on your partner's list. This line can represent how the combination of your two qualities complements one another or works well together.

    Once you have completed Exercise One, ask your partner to offer feedback on his/her perception of these specific qualities. You can do the same for your partner once he/she has completed this section of the workbook.

The goal is to simply have a meaningful discussion about your uniqueness as a couple. Do your best to be open and receptive to feedback—and be graceful and sensitive in your feedback to your partner.

You may want to jot a note or two on the insights you now have as a result of your discussion:

_____

_____

_____

_____

_____

_____

_____

 **EXERCISE**
TASK ORIENTED OR PEOPLE ORIENTED?

Within the personality pinwheel on page 2 of your Deep Love Report, you will find two circles. The outer circle notes "Task Oriented" on the top and "People Oriented" on the bottom. Note which camp you fall into (or maybe you're right on the dividing line).

One is not better than the other. They are just different. Both present challenges and advantages within your relationship. We'll get to those in a moment. For now, simply indicate on this continuum where each of you perceives yourself to be, based on where you are on the personality pinwheel.

The "Achieving Spouse" would be a 3 on the Task Oriented end of this scale. The "Cooperating Spouse" would be a 3 on the People Oriented end.

TASK ORIENTED   PEOPLE ORIENTED

3	2	1	2	3
ACHIEVING	ANALYZING / PIONEERING	DELIBERATING / ENERGIZING	UNWAVERING / AFFIRMING	COOPERATING

The nearer you are to the Task Oriented end of the continuum, the more you prize getting things done. You love an assignment. You probably live by a to-do list. You're gratified by accomplishment—whether solving a minor problem or moving up in your career. You stay on task, and you're probably competitive. Getting a job done, whether big or small, can take priority over other considerations (and sometimes that includes people's feelings).

In fact, anything that stands in your way of getting the task accomplished will likely become a "distraction." You like concrete objectives. You like to measure your progress. Plainly put, you like to be productive.

Now, the nearer you are to the People Oriented end of the continuum, the more likely you are to value the emotional well-being of others over productivity. You're good at working with people, and you're friendly. You get a "feeling" for people early on in a conversation and seem to know just what to say. You're rarely forceful or domineering. You're flexible, and you adapt easily to other people's situations and attitudes. You're diplomatic. You prize consensus and harmony. You're a team player. Nobody would describe you as a loner. In short, you're a "people person."

Of course, you may have qualities from both sides of the continuum—even if you lean heavily to one end or the other.

> Personality has power to uplift, power to depress, power to curse, and power to bless.
>
> *Paul Harris*

The following list contrasts the two ends of the scale. Check a total of three qualities you identify with most. You may choose from either side, but it can only be three qualities in total.

TASK ORIENTED	PEOPLE ORIENTED
☐ Driven	☐ Nurturing
☐ Measurable goals	☐ Heart-felt connections
☐ Work from a to-do list	☐ What to-do list?
☐ Concentrated and focused	☐ Welcome interruptions
☐ Delay gratification	☐ Procrastinate
☐ Make others feel nervous	☐ Make others feel comfortable

As you know, there are no right or wrong answers. Fifty percent of the population falls into each side of this continuum—some people more extreme than others. Take a moment to list two or three real-life and concrete examples that would illustrate the three characteristics you checked:

HIS

1. _____
2. _____
3. _____

HERS

1. _____
2. _____
3. _____

Discuss how your approach—whether it's task oriented, people oriented, or both—has impacted your relationship. Consider both positive and challenging aspects. No need to size up your partner. Simply take time for each of you to share your perception of how this part of your own personality has impacted the relationship. Don't judge or critique each other. Just disclose your personal perspectives about yourselves.

You may want to jot a note or two on the insights you now have as a result of your discussion:

_____

_____

_____

_____

_____

_____

> There is very little difference in people, but that little difference makes a big difference.
>
> *W. Clement Stone*

 **EXERCISE**
SLOWER PACED OR FASTER PACED?

Now shift your attention to the inner circle on the personality pinwheel on page 2 of your Deep Love Report. Which camp do you fall into?

Again, one is not better than the other. Indicate how you perceive yourself to be, based on where you are on the personality pinwheel. Do the same for your partner.

The "Deliberating Spouse" would be a 3 on the Slower Paced end of this scale. The "Energizing Spouse" would be a 3 on the Faster Paced end.

SLOWER PACED   *FASTER PACED*

3	2	1	2	3
DELIBERATING	ANALYZING UNWAVERING	ACHIEVING COOPERATING	PIONEERING AFFIRMING	ENERGIZING

The closer you are to the Slower Paced end of the continuum, the more you take your time. You don't overschedule. You like to linger. If you don't get something done today, you'll get it done tomorrow—or the next day. You move more deliberately. You ponder and muse. You are measured and unhurried. Plainly put, you are slower paced.

The closer you are to the Faster Paced end, the more urgency you embody. You like to get things done *yesterday*! You don't want to waste time. You're ready to get going. You want to use your time wisely. You often measure success in relationship to speed. You can become impatient more easily than others because your days are packed. You schedule things back-to-back. Others are often amazed by how you can get so much done in such a short time. You run on rocket fuel. In short, you're a faster paced person.

Again, you may be somewhere in the middle. Check a total of three qualities you identify with most. You may choose from either side, but it can only be three qualities in total.

SLOWER PACED	FASTER PACED
☐ Unite and concede	☐ Divide and conquer
☐ Patient	☐ Impatient
☐ Ready to rest	☐ Raring to go
☐ Steady and stable	☐ Excited and energetic
☐ Roundabout	☐ To the point
☐ "Think before you act"	☐ "Don't just sit there, do something"
☐ "Slow-growing trees bear the best fruit"	☐ "Early bird gets the worm"

> The goal in marriage is not to think alike, but to think together.
>
> *Robert C. Dodds*

Again, there are no right or wrong answers. Take a moment to list two or three real-life and concrete examples that would illustrate the three characteristics you checked:

HIS

1. _____

_____

2. _____

_____

3. _____

_____

HERS

1. _____

_____

2. _____

_____

3. _____

_____

Discuss how your approach—whether it's slower paced or faster paced—has impacted your relationship. Consider both positive and challenging aspects. Talk about yourself, not your partner (this is not a time for critique).

You may want to jot a note or two on the insights you now have as a result of your discussion:

_____

_____

_____

_____

_____

4 EXERCISE
DIVING DEEPER INTO YOUR PERSONALITY

The lower portion of page 2 on your report provides each of you with a personalized paragraph. This paragraph is unique to you. It's not simply one of eight different paragraphs you might receive based on your personality category; it's much deeper and more sophisticated than that. In fact, if you are both in the same category, your paragraphs will still be unique to each of you.

We recommend the following:

1. Read your paragraph to yourself.

2. Highlight or underline two or three sentences you identify with most.

3. Scratch through any sentence you don't think fits.

4. Read aloud your entire paragraph to your partner.

5. Have him/her do the same for you.

Discuss your two personalized paragraphs with each other. You may want to use these questions to get the conversation going:

1. How accurate would you say your paragraph is on a scale of 1 to 10?

2. How accurate does your partner think your paragraph is?

3. What do you identify with most and why?

4. What do you identify with least and why?

You may want to jot a note or two on the insights you now have as a result of your discussion:

_____

_____

_____

_____

_____

Now read the paragraph at the top of page 3 of your report. It describes how your two personalities work together.

Also, read the list of strengths each of your personalities brings to the relationship. Underline which one of your five you agree with most. Also note which of the five from your partner's list you appreciate the most.

Discuss your combined paragraph—personalized to the two of you. Here are some questions to get you going:

1. How does the combined paragraph make you feel? Why?

_____

_____

2. What new insights does it provide for you? Use examples.

_____

_____

Now talk about what you appreciate most on your partner's list and why you value it in the relationship.

1. Discuss the strengths that each of you brings to the relationship. Explore your top choices. What are they?

_____

_____

2. Why did you select them? Use examples.

_____

_____

You may want to jot a note or two on the insights you now have as a result of your discussion:

_____

_____

_____

_____

_____

5 EXERCISE
YOUR PERSONALITY STYLES

The lower portion of page 3 of your Deep Love Report depicts four important relationship dynamics that are shaped by your personalities.

For each one of these issues, think of a specific example or two in your life as a couple. For example, what would be a recent problem you've tried to solve together? (Consider big problems as well as relatively minor ones.) Think of real-life examples and note them here.

HIS

1. Solving problems:

_____

_____

2. Influencing each other:

_____

_____

3. Reacting to change:

_____

_____

4. Making decisions:

_____

_____

HERS

1. Solving problems:

_____

_____

2. Influencing each other:

_____

_____

3. Reacting to change:

_____

_____

4. Making decisions:

_____

_____

Now consider how your personalities influence the process and outcomes in these areas. Here are some questions to get you started:

1. How does your own personality shape these specific examples?

   _____

   _____

2. How, if at all, would you have liked to approach the issue differently?

   _____

   _____

3. What do you appreciate about your partner's personality in the context of these examples?

   _____

   _____

4. How do your personalities complement one another in these examples?

   _____

   _____

The goal here is to understand how each other is hardwired and appreciate how your partner's personality differences leverage your own.

You may want to jot a note or two on the insights you now have as a result of your discussion:

_____

_____

_____

_____

_____

_____

Each of these four areas represents an emotional safety need within your personality. Here's how it pans out:

- If you're an aggressive problem solver, your safety need is **time**. You prize efficiency with your time, and you feel threatened when it's not being used well.

- If you're influenced more by feelings than facts, **approval** is your safety need. You want to be sure you are on the same team with your partner, and you feel threatened if you're losing his/her approval.

- If you resist change more than you accept it, a deep sense of **predictability** is your safety need. You don't want change without warning, and you feel threatened when it happens.

- If you are more cautious than spontaneous when it comes to decision-making, your safety need is **quality**. You hold high standards for doing the right thing the right way. And when decisions aren't given careful consideration, you feel threatened.

You may have one or more emotional safety needs. Based on your results at the bottom of page 3 of your report, circle the safety needs that apply to you:

HIS	HERS
Time	Time
Approval	Approval
Predictability	Predictability
Quality	Quality

Talk about your emotional safety needs as they relate to the way your personal personality is hardwired. Here are some questions to get you started:

1. How does your safety need seem to be expressed? Be specific and use examples.

_____

_____

2. How can you be more sensitive and caring with your partner's emotional safety need? Again, be specific and use examples.

_____

_____

You may want to jot a note or two on the insights you now have as a result of your discussion:

_____

_____

_____

_____

_____

_____

SESSION TAKEAWAY

Keep the big picture in mind. Heightened self-awareness and mutual empathy are the point of this first session. As a result of your investment in these two pages of your Deep Love Report, you are now more aware of how each other is uniquely hardwired. This makes empathy much easier. The more you understand and appreciate in your differing personalities, the more you increase your inclination to put yourselves in each other's shoes. We'll say it again: Empathy is essential to enjoying deeper love.

THE BOTTOM LINE

The greatest insight I got from this session is . . .

HIS   **HERS**

_____   _____

_____   _____

_____   _____

_____   _____

_____   _____

The one thing I'd like to do differently in our relationship as a result of this session is . . .

HIS   **HERS**

_____   _____

_____   _____

_____   _____

_____   _____

_____   _____

PUTTING IT INTO PRACTICE

Over the next few days, make a conscious effort to intentionally see the world from your partner's perspective.

- Deliberately put yourself in his/her shoes. Imagine what life is like in his/her skin.

- Think about how your partner's emotional safety need influences his/her day and interactions with you.

- Express your appreciation to your partner for what his/her personality contributes to your relationship.

It's all about empathy. And don't forget to review pages 2 and 3 of your Deep Love Report from time to time to help you understand your partner better.

> Empathy deploys a shorthand that gets two people on the same page immediately, without having to waste time or words explaining what matters.
>
> *Darryl McDaniels*

SMALL GROUP EXPERIENCE FOR SESSION ONE:
PERSONALITY

JUST FOR FUN (5 MINUTES)

Think about the first date the two of you shared. Where did you go? What did you do? What's most memorable and why?

BIBLICAL WISDOM (5 MINUTES)

Consider these verses as you begin this session together:

- "Encourage one another and build each other up, just as in fact you are doing." —1 Thessalonians 5:11

- "God has given each of you a gift from his great variety of spiritual gifts. Use them well to serve one another." —1 Peter 4:10 (NLT)

- "Don't look out only for your own interests, but take an interest in others, too." —Philippians 2:4 (NLT)

Which passage do you identify with most or find most challenging? Why? You may want to also begin your session with a word of prayer together, asking God to help each of you see through the eyes of your partner like never before.

VIDEO NOTES (5 MINUTES)

_____

_____

_____

_____

TALKING THROUGH YOUR EXERCISES TOGETHER (40 MINUTES)

Within your small group, discuss the results from the exercises you did as a couple beforehand. And have your Deep Love Report at the ready. Each couple can share what they learned, but feel free to ask questions of each other along the way. No need to make this like a presentation. Keep it relaxed and interactive. Learn from each other. Here are some questions to cover:

- Consider Exercise Two from this session. Are you more task oriented or people oriented? And how has that shaped your relationship with each other?

- Do the same with Exercise Three. Are you slower paced or faster paced? How has this impacted your relationship?

- What do you make of how the report depicts your two personalities? What resonates with you the most and why? Hold up the page depicting where each of you lands on the personality pinwheel so other members of the group can see it. Discuss how you are similar to or different from others in the group.

- Note the individual strengths you bring into your relationship. Better yet, have each partner talk about a specific strength or two that he/she appreciates in his/her partner and explain why (use examples).

- If you're up to it, explore what you learned about your own emotional safety need(s) from Exercise Five. Based on the information gained in this exercise, what makes you feel most secure: time, approval, predictability, or quality?

- Finally, discuss the big picture—mutual empathy. How will you each be more likely to see the world from your partner's point of view after this session? What do you understand better about your partner as a result of these two pages of your Deep Love Report? What's one practical example of how you plan to empathize with your partner in the coming week?

WRAP-UP (5 MINUTES)

Revisit the Biblical Wisdom section of this group session. Someone might read each verse aloud once more. Let them sink in as you close the session in prayer.

> Love is not blind—it sees more, not less. But because it sees more, it is willing to see less.
>
> *Julius Gordon*

SESSION TWO
COMMUNICATION

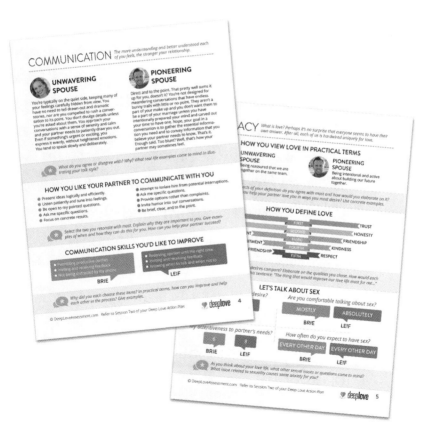

COMMUNICATION *The more understanding and better understood each of you feels, the stronger your relationship.*

UNWAVERING SPOUSE

You're typically on the quiet side, keeping many of your feelings carefully hidden from view. You have no need to tell drawn-out and dramatic stories, nor are you compelled to rush a conversation to its point. You don't divulge details unless you're asked about them. You approach them and your partner needs to patiently draw you out. Even if something's urgent or exciting, you express it evenly, without heightened emotions. You tend to speak slowly and deliberately.

PIONEERING SPOUSE

Direct and to the point. That pretty well sums it up for you, doesn't it? You're not designed for meandering conversations that have endless bunny trails with little or no point. They aren't a part of your make up and you don't want them to be a part of your marriage unless you have intentionally prepared your mind and carved out your time to have one. Nope, your goal in a conversation is to gather the essential information you need and to convey information that you believe your partner needs to know. That's it. Enough said. Too blunt? Well, that's how your partner may sometimes feel.

What do you agree or disagree with? Why? What real life examples come to mind to illustrating your talk style?

HOW YOU LIKE YOUR PARTNER TO COMMUNICATE WITH YOU

- Present ideas logically and efficiently.
- Listen patiently and tune into feelings.
- Be open to my pointed questions.
- Ask me specific questions.
- Focus on concrete results.

- Attempt to isolate him from potential interruptions.
- Ask me specific questions.
- Provide options rather than complaints.
- Invite humor into our conversations.
- Be brief, clear, and to the point.

Select the two you resonate with most. Explain why they are important to you. Give examples of when and how they can do this for you. How can you help your partner succeed?

COMMUNICATION SKILLS YOU'D LIKE TO IMPROVE

- Permitting productive conflict.
- Inviting and receiving feedback
- Not being distracted by my phone

- Reserving opinion until the right time.
- Inviting and receiving feedback
- Knowing when to talk and when not to

BRIE

LEIF

Why did you each choose these items? In practical terms, how can you improve and help each other in the process? Give examples.

© DeepLoveAssessment.com Refer to Session Two of your Deep Love Action Plan

♥ deeplove 4

...ACY *What is love? Perhaps it's no surprise that everyone seems to have their own answer. After all, each of us is hardwired uniquely for love.*

HOW YOU VIEW LOVE IN PRACTICAL TERMS

...UNWAVERING SPOUSE
...eing reassured that we are ...together on the same team.

PIONEERING SPOUSE

Being intentional and active about building our future together.

...ects of your definition do you agree with most and how would you elaborate on it? ...you help your partner love you in ways you most desire? Use concrete examples.

HOW YOU DEFINE LOVE

	FIRST		TRUST
	SECOND		HONESTY
...NT	THIRD		FRIENDSHIP
...ITMENT	FOURTH		KINDNESS
...FRIENDSHIP	FIFTH	RESPECT	

...desires compare? Elaborate on the qualities you chose. How would each ...his sentence: "The thing that would improve our love life most for me..."

LET'S TALK ABOUT SEX

...desire? *Are you comfortable talking about sex?*

| MOSTLY | ABSOLUTELY |

BRIE **LEIF**

...y attentiveness to partner's needs? *How often do you expect to have sex?*

| 6 | 8 |
| BRIE | LEIF |

| EVERY OTHER DAY | EVERY OTHER DAY |
| BRIE | LEIF |

As you think about your love life, what other sexual issues or questions come to mind? What issue related to sexuality causes some anxiety for you?

© DeepLoveAssessment.com Refer to Session Two of your Deep Love Action Plan

♥ deeplove 5

HOW IMPROVING COMMUNICATION LEADS TO DEEP LOVE

Communication—understanding and being understood—is the lifeblood of your relationship. Truly, your love life will sink or swim according to how well you communicate. In fact, your level of physical and emotional intimacy is so intricately entwined with communication that it's impossible to separate them. Love relationships maintain themselves linguistically. Little conversations, piled one on top of the other, can easily tip the scales toward feeling either horribly misunderstood or deeply known and loved.

Your two unique personalities come to conversations with different needs and desires. The more you understand your two talk styles, the more you crack the code for enjoying great conversations and deeper love together.

① EXERCISE
HOW'S YOUR TALK LIFE?

The number one problem couples report in their relationship is predictable: "a breakdown in communication." And with good reason. Whether a relationship succeeds or fails depends on how well partners send and receive messages, how well they use their conversations to understand and be understood.

So how's your talk life? In general, how would you rate it on the following scale? Take a moment to honestly consider your answer.

NOT GREAT   *FANTASTIC*

1   2   3   4   5   6   7   8   9   10

Talk about how satisfied you are currently with your level of communication in your relationship. Use these questions:

- Discuss why you rated your communication level where you did. But steer clear of any potential critical comments about your partner. Focus on what a great conversation looks like for you.

- What do you especially enjoy or appreciate about your current level of communication with each other? Use a specific example.

- Even if you are ranking your current level of communication as very positive, can you imagine it being better?

- How open are you to personally working on your own communication abilities?

You may want to jot a note or two on the insights you now have as a result of your discussion:

_____

_____

_____

_____

_____

_____

> The most important thing in communication is to hear what isn't being said.
>
> *Peter Druker*

② EXERCISE
YOUR PERSONAL TALK STYLES

At the top of page 4 of your Deep Love Report, you'll find two paragraphs describing your two unique talk styles. These factor in your personalities and your unique characteristics.

We recommend the following:

1. Have your partner read your paragraph aloud to you.

2. Have him/her note the two sentences that he/she thinks are most accurate.

3. Highlight or underline two or three sentences you identify with most. Are they the same or different from what your partner selected?

4. Scratch through any sentence that doesn't fit.

Discuss your two paragraphs with each other. You may want to use these questions to get the conversation going:

- How accurate would you say your paragraph is on a scale of 1 to 10?

- How accurate does your partner think your paragraph is?

- What do you identify with most and why?

- What real-life examples come to mind in illustrating your two talk styles?

You may want to jot a note or two on the insights you now have as a result of your discussion:

_____

_____

_____

_____

_____

_____

> A finely tuned ear is at the heart of empathy.
>
> *Daniel Goleman*

③ EXERCISE
GETTING WHAT YOU WANT AND NEED IN CONVERSATIONS

In the middle of page 4 of your Deep Love Report, you'll find two columns of bulleted lists—one for each of you. These lists describe things you'd like most for your partner to do for you in your conversations together.

We recommend the following:

1. Read the list to yourself.

2. Note two items you desire most.

Review your two lists with each other. Begin by reading all five items aloud to your partner. Each of you may want to then use these questions to facilitate the conversation:

- Which two items did you indicate as most important to you? Why?

- What real-life examples come to mind in illustrating your two items?

- What would be the likely result if you received these two desires more frequently from your partner?

You may want to jot a note or two on the insights you had as a result of your discussion:

_____

_____

_____

_____

_____

_____

④ EXERCISE
IMPROVING YOUR TALK SKILLS

Near the bottom of page 4 of your Deep Love Report, you'll find a list of three items you'd like to improve within yourself as you communicate better with your partner.

We recommend the following:

1. Review the lists.

2. Note the one item you want to improve the most from your own list.

Begin by reading the three items on your list aloud to your partner. Use these questions to guide your conversation:

- Which item do you want to improve the most and why?

- What real-life examples come to mind in illustrating how this will look when you begin to improve it? Be as specific as possible.

- What will you do, in specific ways, to actually improve this skill? How would you like your partner to help you improve it?

- How will improving this skill improve your overall communication level?

You may want to jot a note or two on the insights you now have as a result of your discussion:

_____

_____

_____

_____

_____

_____

_____

> An understanding heart is everything
> and cannot be esteemed highly enough.
>
> *Carl Gustav Jung*

 **EXERCISE**
EXPLORING INTIMACY

At the top of page 5 of your Deep Love Report, you'll find a brief description of how each of you views love in practical terms. This is based on your personality.

Review these two brief descriptions with each other. Begin by reading them aloud to each other. Each of you may want to then use these questions to facilitate the conversation:

- How accurately does this capture how you view love? If you need to elaborate or edit the description, feel free. Use it as a way to describe how you view love in practical terms.

- What do you think about your partner's description? Can you think of a recent example of when you loved your partner in this way?

- Keeping these descriptions in mind, how can each of you better love one another? Be as specific with examples as possible.

You may want to jot a note or two on the insights you now have as a result of your discussion:

_____

_____

_____

_____

_____

_____

_____

⑥ EXERCISE
HOW YOU DEFINE LOVE

Everyone has a different priority of ingredients that go into romantic love. In the middle of page 5 of your Deep Love Report, you'll find a hierarchy of ingredients based on how each of you defines love. The better you understand what's important to each of you, the deeper your love can grow.

Review your ingredients of love together. Read them aloud to each other. In fact, you may want to go back and forth, alternating your ingredients as you move down the list together. Use these questions:

- How would you elaborate on your top ingredient, and why is it at the top of your list?

- What questions do you have for your partner regarding his/her top ingredient?

- Can you share examples of what the different ingredients look like?

- What clarifications would be helpful for you? Be sure you understand what your partner means by the terms he/she selected.

You may want to jot a note or two on the insights you now have as a result of your discussion:

_____

_____

_____

_____

_____

_____

> Never miss a good chance to shut up.
>
> *Will Rogers*

 ## EXERCISE
LET'S TALK ABOUT SEX

Talking about sex—even with the person you love the most—can be uncomfortable. But it's essential to improving your sex life together. The lower portion of page 5 of your Deep Love Report depicts your individual answers to four fundamental questions. The more you are able to talk comfortably with each other about these, the more connected you will be.

Look at each of the four questions and your individual answers. Focus on one at a time and read them aloud. For each of the four questions and answers, discuss using these questions:

- Does how your partner answered surprise you in any way? Why or why not?
- How do you feel about each other's answers?
- What can you do—in practical terms—to improve in this area? Be specific.

You may want to jot a note or two on the insights you now have as a result of your discussion:

_____

_____

_____

_____

_____

_____

SESSION TAKEAWAY

Keep the big picture in mind. Communication is the lifeblood of your relationship. You need to continually take great care to keep it healthy.

You're now both more aware of your individual talk styles and can better appreciate one another's communication needs. The more effectively you meet those needs, the more intimacy, romance, and closeness you'll experience together. In short, the better you communicate, the deeper your love.

> Good communication is as stimulating as black coffee.
>
> *Anne Morrow Lindbergh*

THE BOTTOM LINE

The greatest insight I got from this session is . . .

HIS

_____

_____

_____

_____

_____

_____

HERS

_____

_____

_____

_____

_____

_____

The one thing I'd like to do differently in our relationship as a result of this session is . . .

HIS

HERS

_____ _____

_____ _____

_____ _____

_____ _____

_____ _____

_____ _____

PUTTING IT INTO PRACTICE

Over the next few days, make a conscious effort to intentionally put into practice the communication skills and insights you learned in this session.

- Deliberately think about how your partner is hardwired for conversation and do what you can to accommodate it.

- Think back to the previous session and consider your partner's emotional safety need and how you can better meet it to improve your communication patterns.

- Take a mental note each day this week of how your partner views intimacy and love and do something intentional to better love him/her.

Again, understanding each other's talk styles and romantic needs helps you better empathize. So review pages 4 and 5 of your Deep Love Report on occasion to help you see the world from your partner's perspective.

> Sometimes sex is great; sometimes sex is kind of so-so; sometimes you'd rather have ice cream and watch television.
>
> *Marty Klein*

SMALL GROUP EXPERIENCE FOR SESSION TWO:
COMMUNICATION

JUST FOR FUN (5 MINUTES)

Describe a time when you surprised your partner. What did you do? Was it romantic? Comical? Scary?

BIBLICAL WISDOM (5 MINUTES)

Consider these verses as you begin this session together:

- "A word fitly spoken is like apples of gold in a setting of silver." —Proverbs 25:11 (ESV)

- "Do not let any unwholesome talk come out of your mouths, but only what is helpful for building others up according to their needs, that it may benefit those who listen." —Ephesians 4:29

- "Let your conversation be always full of grace, seasoned with salt, so that you may know how to answer everyone." —Colossians 4:6

Which passage do you identify with most or find most challenging? Why? You may want to also begin your session with a word of prayer together, asking God to help each of you see what you can personally do to become a better communicator in your relationship.

VIDEO NOTES (5 MINUTES)

_____

_____

_____

_____

TALKING THROUGH YOUR EXERCISES TOGETHER (40 MINUTES)

Within your small group, discuss the results from the exercises you did as a couple beforehand. And have your Deep Love Report at the ready. Each couple can share what they learned, but feel free to ask questions of each other along the way. No need to make this like a presentation. Keep it relaxed and interactive. Learn from each other. Here are some questions to cover:

- Consider Exercise Two from this session, on your personal talk styles. What resonated most with you from your descriptive paragraph in the report? Why?

- Consider Exercise Three. What do you want and need most from your partner when it comes to communication? Why? Do others in your group identify with the same issue?

- What did you learn about your partner from page 4 of your Deep Love Report? What will you personally do with this new insight to improve the communication between the two of you?

- When it comes to something specific that you'd like to improve in your communication skills (see the bottom of page 4 of your report), which one will you choose? Why? What will you do, in practical terms, to improve it this week?

- Note how your partner tends to view love (see the top of page 5 of your report). With this understanding about your partner, what will you do to convey love in concrete terms in the coming days? Use examples. Are you open to suggestions from others in your group on this front?

- Keeping the big picture in mind, how will your new insights into one another's communication needs and abilities help each of you practice more empathy for each other? Give some concrete examples. What can you learn from other couples in the group about this?

WRAP-UP (5 MINUTES)

Revisit the Biblical Wisdom section of this group session. Someone might read each verse aloud once more. Let them sink in as you close the session in prayer.

SESSION THREE
CONFLICT

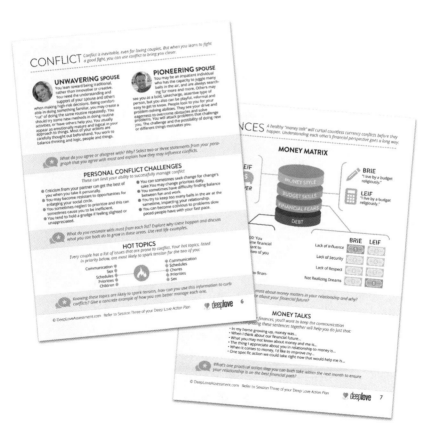

CONFLICT *Conflict is inevitable, even for loving couples. But when you learn to fight a good fight, you can use conflict to bring you closer.*

UNWAVERING SPOUSE
You lean toward being traditional, rather than innovative or creative. You need the understanding and support of your spouse and others when making high-risk decisions. Being comfortable in doing something familiar, you may create a "rut" of doing the same routine repeatedly. You should try some new methods in doing routine activities, or have others help you. You usually appear as emotionally mature and logical in your approach to things. Most of your actions are carefully thought out beforehand. You work to balance thinking and logic, people and things.

PIONEERING SPOUSE
You may be an impatient individual who has the capacity to juggle many balls in the air, and are always searching for more and more. Others may see you as a bold, take-charge, assertive type of person, but you also can be playful, informal and easy to get to know. People look to you for your problem-solving abilities. They see your drive and eagerness to overcome obstacles and solve problems. You will attack problems that challenge you. The challenge and the possibility of doing new or different things motivates you.

What do you agree or disagree with? Why? Select two or three statements from your paragraph that you agree with most and explain how they may influence conflicts.

PERSONAL CONFLICT CHALLENGES
These can limit your ability to successfully manage conflict

- Criticism from your partner can get the best of you when you take it personally.
- You may become resistant to opportunities for enlarging your social circle.
- You sometimes neglect to prioritize and this can sometimes cause you to be inefficient.
- You tend to hold a grudge if feeling slighted or unappreciated.

- You can sometimes seek change for change's sake. You may change priorities daily.
- You sometimes have difficulty finding balance between fun and work.
- You try to keep too many balls in the air at the sometime, impacting your relationship.
- You can become oblivious to problems slow paced people have with your fast pace.

What do you resonate with most from each list? Explore why these happen and discuss what you can both do to grow in these areas. Use real life examples.

HOT TOPICS
Every couple has a list of issues that are prone to conflict. Your hot topics, listed in priority below, are most likely to spark tension for the two of you:

Communication — Communication
Sex — Schedules
Schedules — Chores
Priorities — Priorities
Children — Sex

Knowing these topics are likely to spark tension, how can you use this information to curb conflicts? Give a concrete example of how you can better manage each one.

© DeepLoveAssessment.com Refer to Session Three of your Deep Love Action Plan   ♥ deeplove   6

...NCES *A healthy "money talk" will curtail countless currency conflicts before they happen. Understanding each other's financial perspective goes a long way.*

MONEY MATRIX

MONEY STYLE
BUDGET SKILLS
FINANCIAL FEARS
DEBT

BRIE
"I live by a budget religiously."

LEIF
"I live by a budget religiously."

	BRIE	LEIF
Lack of Influence		
Lack of Security		
Lack of Respect		
Not Realizing Dreams		

...most about money matters in your relationship and why? ...e about your financial future?

MONEY TALKS
...finances, you'll want to keep the communication ...completing these sentences together will help you do just that:

- In my home growing up, money was...
- When I think about our financial future...
- What you may not know about money and me is...
- The thing I appreciate about you in relationship to money is...
- When it comes to money, I'd like to improve my...
- One specific action we could take right now that would help me is...

What's one practical action step you can both take within the next month to ensure your relationship is in the best financial path?

© DeepLoveAssessment.com Refer to Session Three of your Deep Love Action Plan   ♥ deeplove   7

THE BIG PICTURE

HOW MANAGING CONFLICT LEADS TO DEEP LOVE

Let's be honest. It doesn't matter how loving you may be, conflict is inevitable. No couple is immune. We argue about small nagging things as well as major issues. A tug-of-war of some kind, even in loving relationships, is common and normal. Little scrapes, spats, and squabbles are endemic.

But here's the good news. Conflict can bring you closer. Conflict, in fact, is the price we pay for a deeper level of connection. It's true. If you learn to fight a "good fight," it deepens your love for each other.

What matters is *how* we fight—the quality of our quarreling—not *whether* we fight. That's why we'll be looking at your personalities once more in this session and how the two of you can best manage conflict together—especially when it comes to money. After all, finances are the number one source of conflict for most couples. Whether you have tension over money or not, getting a better grip on conflict will improve your financial conversations. You'll also deepen your love for each other in the process.

1 EXERCISE
WHAT ARE YOUR FIGHT TYPES?

It's impossible to separate your personality from the way you manage conflict. At the top of page 6 of your Deep Love Report, you'll see a paragraph for each of you. It describes your fight type.

We recommend the following:

1. Read your paragraph to yourself.

2. Highlight or underline two or three sentences you identify with most.

3. Scratch through any sentence you don't think fits.

4. Read aloud your entire paragraph to your partner.

5. Have him/her do the same for you.

Discuss your two personalized paragraphs with each other. Consider these questions:

- How accurate would you say your paragraph is on a scale of 1 to 10?

- How accurate does your partner think your paragraph is?

- What do you identify with most and why?

- What do you identify with least and why?

- What real-life examples come to mind in illustrating your two approaches to managing conflict?

- Think of a time when you managed conflict well and a time when you could have used some help. What made the difference?

You may want to jot a note or two on the insights you now have as a result of your discussion:

_____

_____

_____

_____

_____

_____

_____

Whenever you're in conflict with someone, there is one factor that can make the difference between damaging your relationship and deepening it. That factor is attitude.

William James

② EXERCISE
YOUR PERSONAL CONFLICT CHALLENGES

Everyone has areas to improve upon when it comes to conflict. In the middle of page 6 of your Deep Love Report, you'll find a list of four items that would likely improve your capacity to manage conflict.

We recommend the following:

1. Read the list to yourself.

2. Note the two items you want to improve the most.

💬 Review your two lists with each other. Begin by reading all four items on your list aloud to your partner. Use these questions to guide your conversation:

- Which item would you like to improve the most and why?

- What real-life examples come to mind in illustrating how this will look when you begin to improve it? Be as specific as possible.

- What will you do, in specific ways, to actually improve in this area? How would you like your partner to help you improve it?

- How will improving this skill improve your overall ability as a couple to manage conflicts?

You may want to jot a note or two on the insights you now have as a result of your discussion:

_____

_____

_____

_____

_____

_____

_____

> Conflict provides an opportunity to love your mate in the midst of difficult circumstances.
>
> *Toben Heim*

 EXERCISE
YOUR HOT TOPICS

Becoming more conscious of what conflictual issues seem to surface most in your relationship can be especially helpful. Why? Because then you can do something to diminish conflicts around those topics. Most couples, after all, have trigger issues that seem to generate more heat than they should. And the sooner you identify your hot topics, the sooner you'll be able to cool off when one of them flames up.

Review your hot topics with each other. Begin by reading all five items on your personal lists aloud to each other. Use these questions to guide your conversation:

- What real-life examples come to mind in illustrating why some of the issues are on this list? As a reminder, steer clear of critiquing each other here. Stay positive and learn from what you've experienced.

- Do you have items that are on both of your lists? If so, these may be the ones you'll want to tackle first. What can you do to improve what you both do when these items come up? Be specific. What's your practical action plan?

- How will your action plan work in specific terms, and what does a successful outcome look like to each of you?

You may want to jot a note or two on the insights you now have as a result of your discussion:

_____

_____

_____

_____

_____

_____

④ EXERCISE
YOUR MONEY MATRIX

Couples fight more about money than about children, chores, work, or friends. Couples fight about money, on average, three times per month. Whether it's about unexpected expenses or insufficient savings, *how* a couple manages money squabbles is a strong predictor of a couple's stability.

Despite all the conflict couples have over money, 55 percent of couples do not set aside time on a regular basis to talk about financial issues. That's why we are devoting this section of the Deep Love experience to this issue.

The top half of page 7 reveals your Money Matrix—four important dimensions for how the two of you approach money:

1. Money Style
2. Budget Skills
3. Financial Fears
4. Debt

Let's take a look at each of them.

MONEY STYLE

More often than not, we tend to match up with our financial opposite. If you're a "saver," your partner will tend to be a "spender" and vice versa. Of course, this is not always the case, but it's the most common. So take a moment to discuss this portion of your Money Matrix.

By talking through your money styles to-gether, you begin to get a better grasp of how they are shaping your interactions. It's especially important to maintain a kind and understanding attitude here. Don't allow negativity to creep into your conversation. Use these questions to guide your conversation:

- What are some specific examples that illustrate your own money style?

- What would happen in your relationship if each of you were the opposite money style of what you are currently? How would your dynamic together differ?

- When your money styles clash, how do you bend a bit to find a middle ground? What makes this especially tough for you to do? Use concrete examples.

- What do you appreciate about your part-ner's money style and why?

You may want to jot a note or two on the insights you now have as a result of your discussion:

_____

_____

_____

_____

_____

_____

_____

> Love is not something people feel,
> but something people try to express
> no matter how they feel.
>
> *Frank Pittman*

BUDGET SKILLS

Now take a look at your budget skills. Are your current approaches working for the two of you? Let's be honest, handling a budget is not everyone's cup of tea. But it's a skill that can be learned and improved if you are motivated.

Working with a budget comes easier for some than others. But every money expert will tell you it's worth the effort to smooth out financial wrinkles in your relationship. Consider these questions:

- How competent do you feel in establishing and working within a budget?

- How satisfied, on a scale of 1 to 10, are you right now with your current approach to budgeting as a couple? Why?
- If you are not satisfied with your current approach, what can you do—starting this week—to improve or remedy the situation? What are the first three steps you need to take?

You may want to jot a note or two on the insights you now have as a result of your discussion:

_____

_____

_____

_____

_____

_____

_____

If you need help in establishing a budget together, you may find it helpful to download a sample budget worksheet at deeploveassessment .com/downloads.

FINANCIAL FEARS

Have you ever considered your financial fears? You'll see that your Money Matrix reveals each of you has one of these four:

1. Lack of Influence—not having a say in your financial approach

2. Lack of Security—not having enough to live on or enough for emergencies

3. Lack of Respect—not receiving respect from your partner on finances

4. Not Realizing Dreams—not being able to do what you want in the future

Money often represents power and control in a relationship. Therefore, the deeper you understand each other's financial fear, the more respect you'll have for one another in this area. Consider these questions:

- Elaborate on your financial fear. Where do you think it comes from, and why is it important to you?

- What can each of you do to soothe one another's level of anxiety around your individual fear? Be specific and concrete.

You may want to jot a note or two on the insights you now have as a result of your discussion:

_____

_____

_____

_____

> If we manage conflict constructively,
> we harness its energy for
> creativity and development.
>
> *Kenneth Kaye*

DEBT

The last piece of your Money Matrix focuses on debt. Whether it's from school loans, a mortgage, car loans, credit cards, or something else, the vast majority of couples have debt. In fact, a third of couples go into debt to pay for their wedding right out of the gate. Of course, it doesn't end there. So what about the two of you? Talking about debt is not fun for most of us, but it's a critical topic for every couple who wants to improve their relationship.

 Debt is a major source of conflict for couples. Consider these questions:

- How comfortable are you with your current level of debt? Why? How is your debt impacting you personally in specific terms? How is it impacting your relationship?

- How are you feeling about your plan to pull together, dig out of it, and stay out of debt? What do you need to do that you're not already doing?

You may want to jot a note or two on the insights you now have as a result of your discussion:

_____

_____

_____

_____

_____

_____

_____

> Peace is not the absence of conflict but the presence of creative alternatives for responding to conflict.
>
> *Dorothy Thompson*

 ## EXERCISE
MONEY TALKS

One of the main reasons couples have financial friction is because they don't routinely talk about money. That's why we've built into your report one of the most effective and time-tested exercises on the topic. You'll find it at the bottom of page 7 of your report.

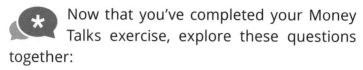 Now that you've completed your Money Talks exercise, explore these questions together:

- What's the biggest insight you learned about yourself and about your partner while doing this exercise?

- How will this new insight shape your attitudes or actions on money going forward?

You may want to jot a note or two on the insights you now have as a result of your discussion:

_____

_____

_____

_____

_____

_____

SESSION TAKEAWAY

For the vast majority of couples, conflict is inevitable. It's not something to ignore or pretend doesn't exist. Conflict is a part of even the most loving relationships. The key is how we manage it. Now that you have a deeper understanding of one another's fight types, you have some new and practical ways to better handle friction in your relationship. You also know what topics are the most heated for you. On top of all this, you've explored your personal Money Matrix and even know what one another's financial fear is. All of this will help you step into each other's shoes and practice deeper intimacy.

THE BOTTOM LINE

The greatest insight I got from this session is . . .

HIS   **HERS**

_____   _____

_____   _____

_____   _____

_____   _____

The one thing I'd like to do differently in our relationship as a result of this session is . . .

HIS   **HERS**

_____   _____

_____   _____

_____   _____

_____   _____

PUTTING IT INTO PRACTICE

Over the next few days, pay attention to even your small squabbles and minor tiffs.

- When you feel yourself becoming frustrated with your partner, consider your two personalities and how you each handle conflict. Heighten your awareness of your partner's experience in this area.

- Consider what you can do to bring the level of tension down for your partner so that the potential conflict becomes more of a discussion than a fight.

- Put some practical guardrails around your hot topics. Solve some problems before they even start by making some decisions ahead of time.

As always, remember the power of empathy—especially in times of conflict. Reviewing pages 6 and 7 of your Deep Love Report from time to time will help you do just that.

SMALL GROUP EXPERIENCE FOR SESSION THREE:
CONFLICT

JUST FOR FUN (5 MINUTES)

If you could have any singer or musical group perform at your partner's next birthday party, who would it be and what song would you have them sing? Why?

BIBLICAL WISDOM (5 MINUTES)

Consider these verses as you begin this session together:

- "A gentle answer turns away wrath, but a harsh word stirs up anger." —Proverbs 15:1

- "In your anger do not sin: Do not let the sun go down while you are still angry." —Ephesians 4:26

- "Love is patient, love is kind." —1 Corinthians 13:4

Which passage do you identify with most or find most challenging and why? You may want to also begin your session with a word of prayer together, asking God to help each of you manage conflict more effectively.

VIDEO NOTES (5 MINUTES)

_____

_____

_____

_____

TALKING THROUGH YOUR EXERCISES TOGETHER (40 MINUTES)

Within your small group, discuss the results from the exercises you did as a couple beforehand. As always, have your Deep Love Report at the ready. Each couple can share what they learned, but feel free to ask questions of each other along the way. No need to make this like a presentation. Keep it relaxed and interactive. Learn from each other. Here are some questions to cover:

- Consider Exercise One from this session, on your personal fight types. What resonated with you most from your descriptive paragraph on the report? Why?

- What did you learn about your partner from the descriptive paragraph about his/her fight type? What will you personally do with this new insight to improve the way you manage conflict?

- Consider Exercise Two. Which of your personal conflict challenges do you want to improve the most and why? What's one thing you can do, in concrete and practical terms, to improve it?

- Consider Exercise Three, regarding your hot topics. Any surprises here? Why or why not? How might your personal conflict challenges relate to your hot topics? Select one of your hot topics together. What can you both do to keep it from heating up so much? Be specific.

- Within your personal Money Matrix, how have your two money styles impacted your relationship? How have they worked for you and against you? What about your financial fears? Can you talk about them and why you might have them?

- Debrief the Money Talks exercise that you did on page 7 of the report. What did you learn about your partner and about yourself as a result of this exercise? How will it help you empathize with each other better?

WRAP-UP (5 MINUTES)

Revisit the Biblical Wisdom section of this group session. Someone might read each verse aloud once more. Let them sink in as you close the session in prayer.

> A nickel ain't worth a dime anymore.
>
> *Yogi Berra*

SESSION FOUR

ADAPTABILITY

THE BIG PICTURE

HOW ADAPTABILITY LEADS TO DEEP LOVE

No relationship—no matter how good—is immune to everyday problems. Some problems quietly sneak up on us without a whisper. Others are about as subtle as a military band. However they arrive, each and every couple suffers unexpected problems and pitfalls.

Life is chock-full of bad situations that are beyond our control. And how a couple responds to these tough times makes all the difference. It comes down to an attitude of adaptability. This attitude supersedes your past, your education, your money, and your circumstances. Why? Because while you can't change your circumstances, you can always change your attitude. The happiest couples don't have a certain set of circumstances, they have a certain attitude: adaptability.

That's why we dedicate this session to helping you rise above whatever challenges you encounter. It's also why we explore your personal time styles. Time is a major issue for most couples, and adaptability has a lot to do with effectively managing it together—and growing deeper in your love.

① EXERCISE
YOUR CURRENT ADAPTABILITY SCORE

At the top of page 8 of your report, you will find your two percentile scores and a brief descriptive paragraph—one for each of you. These reflect how optimistic and resilient you are when faced with a challenge. We provide a percentile number simply as a general look at your adaptability. It's designed to improve your self-awareness (not give you a grade). Don't use this measurement against one another. If you do, you'll miss the point. Think of it as looking in the mirror to see what you might want to change or improve.

We recommend the following:

1. Keep an open and receptive mind to this feedback.

2. Read your own descriptive paragraph to yourself.

3. Note how you feel after reading it.

4. Read your descriptive paragraphs aloud for each other.

Review your two descriptions and your percentiles with each other. Take care and caution to keep from comparing your results here. This is not a competition, so don't read much into having a higher or lower score than your partner.

The percentile is simply a rough gauge to help you each gain a bit of self-awareness. Use these questions to guide your conversation:

- Do you generally agree with your percentile score and your paragraph? Why or why not? Use examples.

- Do you generally agree with your partner's percentile score and his/her paragraph? Why or why not?

- What emotions do you have when you read this information about your current adaptability levels?

- Describe a tough circumstance that you've had to handle and how you coped with it. Were you able to maintain an adaptable and optimistic attitude? If not, what was your biggest challenge preventing that?

- When it comes to being adaptable to circumstances beyond your control, how would you like to respond differently?

All that a man achieves and all that he fails to achieve is the direct result of his own thoughts.

James Allen

You may want to jot a note or two on the insights you now have as a result of your discussion:

_____

_____

_____

_____

_____

_____

2 **EXERCISE**
WHEN YOU FACE A CHALLENGE

In the middle of page 8 of your report, you will find a list of five items describing your general coping tendencies when life becomes particularly demanding.

We recommend the following:

1. Read your list and circle the two that you agree with most.

2. Underline the one that you think is least accurate.

3. Read your lists aloud for each other.

Review your individual lists with each other. Consider these questions together:

- Which two items do you see as being most accurate for you and why? Use examples in your answer.

- Which two items from your partner's list do you think are most accurate for him/her? Does your partner agree with you? Why or why not?

- Do any items seem inaccurate to you from either of your lists? If so, why?

- What do you wish was on your personal list that may not be there and why?

You may want to jot a note or two on the insights you now have as a result of your discussion:

_____

_____

_____

_____

_____

_____

_____

③ EXERCISE
HOW YOUR PARTNER PERCEIVES YOU UNDER STRESS

At the bottom of page 8 of your report, you will find three ways your partner is likely to see you when you are under stress.

We recommend the following:

1. Review your list and your partner's list.

2. Note which item from your partner's list you agree with most.

3. Read your lists aloud for each other.

 Review your three items with each other. Consider these questions together:

- What item from your partner's list do you agree with most and why? As always, use a concrete example.

- How do you feel when your partner exhibits this quality?

- Do any items seem inaccurate to you from either of your lists? If so, why?

- As the two of you together consider all of the information on page 8 of your report, what do you make of your capacity as a couple to adjust to things beyond your control? If you could improve one thing in this area, what would it be and why?

- How can you improve your adaptability to-gether as a couple? What concrete steps can you take here? Can you think of a specific challenge you're currently facing where you can practice your new adaptability insights?

You may want to jot a note or two on the in-sights you now have as a result of your discussion:

_____

_____

_____

_____

_____

_____

 **EXERCISE**
SCHEDULED OR UNSCHEDULED?

In the rat race to get ahead, or just to keep up, we too often neglect what makes life worth living: our relationships—especially our marriage. Life in the fast lane inevitably means less time with the one you love. Where does it go? We try to make it. Save it. Seize it. Buy it. And borrow it. We even try to steal it. And yet time continues to elude us—until we become aware of our two time styles. That's when we begin to recover the moments we've been missing together.

At the top of page 9 of your Deep Love Report, you will find a diagram with a white cross in the middle of it. It represents two axis points, and the horizontal crossbar marks whether you are more scheduled or unscheduled.

We recommend you explore the diagram to see which side of that horizontal continuum you lean into. Do you agree? How about your partner?

Keep in mind that one of these is not better or worse than the other. They just are. Each of us is hardwired differently in our relationship to time. So set aside the temptation to think one is better than the other. They both have good points and challenges, but what we are concerned with is understanding where each of you lands between these two poles. For it is indeed a continuum. Some people are on one extreme or the other, either hard or soft in measuring time, while others are somewhere in between.

Once you've identified which side of the continuum you're on, consider these questions together:

- Do you agree with how you are being identified as scheduled or unscheduled? Why or why not? Can you come up with a concrete example or two that illustrate where you land? Can your partner?

- How might your two approaches on this continuum—whether they are the same or different—impact your relationship? Consider something as common as what it means to be "on time" to each of you. Are you in agreement or not and why?

You may want to jot a note or two on the insights you now have as a result of your discussion:

_____

_____

_____

_____

_____

_____

> You are only one thought away
> from a good feeling.
>
> *Sheila Krystal*

 **EXERCISE**
FUTURE OR PRESENT?

In determining your individual time styles, we also take into consideration whether you are oriented more in the here-and-now or the there-and-then.

Are you energized more about what's taking place in the present or the future?

If you put more energy into what's around the corner than you do into what's happening right now, if you set specific goals, and if you ponder how a financial decision today will impact what you can do tomorrow, you're likely future oriented. If the opposite is true on these questions, you're probably present oriented.

Some of us hardly give a thought to what's next. The time is now. Right now. We're immersed in what's going on in the present. We don't worry much about the future. That only spoils the present. We'd rather seize the moment. And we can't imagine living life any other way. On the other hand, some of us are perplexed and baffled that anyone could do just that. *How do they get anything done?* we wonder. How could they not plan for what's about to happen? Why aren't they more strategic about getting where they want to go?

Again, some people are on one extreme or the other, either focused on today or focused on tomorrow, while many are somewhere in between. The diagram on page 9 of your Deep Love Report shows you where you are, this time on a vertical crossbar.

Once more, we recommend you explore the diagram to see which side of that vertical continuum you lean into. Do you agree? How about your partner?

Once you've identified which end of the continuum you're on, consider these questions together:

- Do you agree with how you are being identified as future oriented or present oriented? Why or why not? Can you give any real-life examples?

- How might your two approaches on this continuum—whether they are the same or different—impact your relationship? Consider something as common as how you approach getting ready for a vacation.

You may want to jot a note or two on the insights you now have as a result of your discussion:

_____

_____

_____

_____

_____

_____

_____

_____

⑥ EXERCISE
YOUR TIME STYLES

Now that you have identified where you land within the crossbar of the diagram at the top of page 9 of your Deep Love Report, you've probably already seen that this results in your time style. You're either an Accommodator, a Processor, a Planner, or a Dreamer. Each has its own strengths, drawbacks, and challenges. Peruse these within the diagram, and then read your personalized time style descriptors on the lower portion of the page.

We recommend the following:

1. Read your paragraph to yourself.

2. Highlight or underline two or three sentences you identify with most.

3. Scratch through any sentence you don't think fits.

4. Read aloud your entire paragraph to your partner.

5. Have him/her do the same for you.

> The supreme happiness of life is the conviction of being loved; loved for yourself, or, more correctly speaking, loved in spite of yourself.
>
> *Victor Hugo*

Discuss your two personalized paragraphs with each other. Consider these questions:

- How accurate would you say your paragraph is on a scale of 1 to 10?

- How accurate does your partner think your paragraph is?

- What do you identify with most and why?

- What do you identify with least and why?

- What contributed to shaping your time style—the home you grew up in, your personality, or something else?

- What real-life examples come to mind in illustrating your two approaches to time?

- How can identifying your time styles help you both value and appreciate what each person brings to the relationship? And how might this knowledge help you have more grace for each other?

You may want to jot a note or two on the insights you now have as a result of your discussion:

_____

_____

_____

_____

SESSION TAKEAWAY

We wish we could put it in a box and give it to you—the capacity to adjust to things beyond your control. Think of the difference it would make in your relationship! We obviously can't do that, but pages 8 and 9 of your report come pretty close. You not only have a new understanding of your time styles, but you now have a new self-awareness when it comes to adaptability, resiliency, and optimism. You now know exactly what you tend to do when faced with a challenge and how your partner perceives you under stress. This awareness is powerful. It allows you to choose a better path—one that will help you rise above circumstances and love each other even when the road gets rocky. And it will. No couple is exempt from encountering bad things. And the better you handle tough times, the deeper your love grows.

> What is the difference between an obstacle and an opportunity? Our attitude toward it. Every opportunity has a difficulty and every difficulty has an opportunity.
>
> *J. Sidlow Baxter*

THE BOTTOM LINE

The greatest insight I got from this session is . . .

HIS   **HERS**

_____   _____

_____   _____

_____   _____

_____   _____

_____   _____

The one thing I'd like to do differently in our relationship as a result of this session is . . .

HIS   **HERS**

_____   _____

_____   _____

_____   _____

_____   _____

_____   _____

Make not your thoughts your prisons.

William Shakespeare

PUTTING IT INTO PRACTICE

Note what struggles or challenges you're experiencing right now—whether big or little.

- Now consider how your partner is experiencing these challenges. See it from his/her perspective.

- Think of ways you can personally manage these challenges better. What's one thing you would change in your attitude or outlook to alter the mood in your relationship?

- When it comes to how the two of you approach time, consider one practical behavior change you can make this coming week to enjoy more quality time together as a couple.

As you conclude this final session, review your entire Deep Love Report for a couple minutes. What are the most important insights you're both taking away from your Deep Love experience?

SMALL GROUP EXPERIENCE FOR SESSION FOUR:
ADAPTABILITY

JUST FOR FUN (5 MINUTES)

Have you studied your partner's funny bone? What's one thing you can always say or do to get a laugh out of your partner?

BIBLICAL WISDOM (5 MINUTES)

Consider these verses as you begin this session together:

- "I have learned to be content whatever the circumstances. I know what it is to be in need, and I know what it is to have plenty. I have learned the secret of being content in any and every situation, whether well fed or hungry, whether living in plenty or in want. I can do all this through him who gives me strength." —Philippians 4:11–13

- "Do not conform to the pattern of this world, but be transformed by the renewing of your mind. Then you will be able to test and approve what God's will is—his good, pleasing and perfect will." —Romans 12:2

- "Be strong and courageous. Do not be afraid or terrified because of them, for the Lᴏʀᴅ your God goes with you; he will never leave you nor forsake you." —Deuteronomy 31:6

Which passage do you identify with most or find most challenging and why? You may want to also begin your session with a word of prayer together, asking God to help each of you learn better how to adjust to things beyond your control.

VIDEO NOTES (5 MINUTES)

_____

_____

_____

_____

TALKING THROUGH YOUR EXERCISES TOGETHER (40 MINUTES)

Within your small group, discuss the results from the exercises you did as a couple beforehand. As always, have your Deep Love Report at the ready. And as you know by now, each couple can share what they learned, but feel free to ask questions of each other along the way. No need to make this like a presentation. Keep it relaxed and interactive. Learn from each other. Here are some questions to cover:

- Consider Exercise Two from this session. What did you learn about yourself here? Of the five listed characteristics that depict what you are like when faced with a challenge, which one do you identify with most? Why? Can you give a specific example?

- What do you think about the list of three items from Exercise Three that may characterize how your partner perceives you when you are under stress? Do you think this is accurate? Why or why not? Do you identify with others in your group on this? What can you learn from each other?

- Consider having your group divide into two subgroups for a moment: those who are unscheduled and those who are scheduled. What does each group feel the other group needs to know about them and why?

- How about another quick division into two subgroups of future oriented and present oriented? Again, see what you each feel the other group needs to know about you and why.

- Take a moment for each couple to share their two time styles with the rest of the group. Talk about what each of the four quadrants is like from your own experience.

Invite other couples to speak into the combination of your two time styles as a couple. What can you learn from each other?

- Keep the big picture in mind for this session—how your capacity to adjust to things beyond your control will impact your relationship, and how understanding your two approaches to time will shape the time you have together. How do you see each of these important topics enabling the two of you to get better at empathy and, in the end, enjoy deeper love?

WRAP-UP (5 MINUTES)

Revisit the Biblical Wisdom section of this group session. Someone might read each verse aloud once more. Let them sink in as you close the session in prayer.

GOING DEEPER

HARMONY

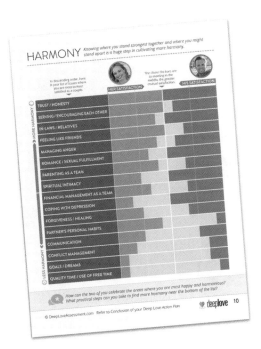

THE BIG PICTURE

HOW CREATING HARMONY LEADS TO DEEP LOVE

The final section of your Deep Love Report helps the two of you consider a strategic next-step plan for taking what you've gained in this experience to an even deeper level. It has to do with the experience of harmony in your relationship. The more content you feel in various areas of your relationship, the more harmony you experience as a couple.

Page 10 of your report reveals a list of the most common challenges or issues couples encounter—everything from "quality time" to "managing anger." It also reveals which of these items the two of you are feeling good about as well as the areas where you are feeling challenged. In fact, this page customizes the list to the two of you. At the top of the list you'll find the issues that are already contributing to your harmony. As you near the bottom of the list, you'll find the issues that are causing you to feel most out of sync with one another.

① EXERCISE
CHARTING YOUR RELATIONSHIP

Before you even get into the details of page 10, we recommend that you first do this quick exercise.

1. The line below represents the length of your relationship up to now.

|——————————————————————————————————|

2. Note different seasons or passages of time on this line. For example, if you've been married for twenty years or so, you might note five-year increments along the line. If you've been together just a handful of years, you might note one-year increments.

3. Next, give a label or identifier to each of the passages. You might call one passage "The Detroit Years" because you lived there during that season. Or another might be "The Toddler Years" or "The Graduate School Years." Give each passage a name that makes sense to the two of you.

4. Now rate your level of satisfaction, content-ment, or happiness on a scale of 1 to 10 during each of these passages.

5. Here's another line representing the future years of your relationship. Again, note some passages—this time, the ones you hope for and dream about.

├───┤

This simple exercise will help you see the com-plete time line of your relationship—where you've come from and where you hope to go together. It gives perspective and will set the stage for the second exercise in this session.

> The surest measure of a man's or a woman's maturity is the harmony, style, joy, and dignity he creates in his marriage.
>
> *Benjamin Spock*

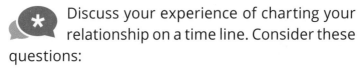 Discuss your experience of charting your relationship on a time line. Consider these questions:

- Discuss your individual ratings of the various passages describing your history together. Why did you rate them the way you did? What can you learn from those passages, especially as it relates to where you'd like to be in the future as a couple?

- What saddens you about your history? What passage from your history do you cherish or celebrate most? Why?

- When you chart your future together, what excites you most and why? Paint a detailed word picture of your future together.

- What can you do today that will help you realize your specific dreams for tomorrow? Don't focus exclusively on financial matters (as important as they are). Consider relationship issues too. What will the two of you need to get better at as a couple to ensure happiness in the future?

You may want to jot a note or two on the insights you now have as a result of your discussion:

_____

_____

_____

② EXERCISE
REVIEWING YOUR HARMONY LIST

The word *harmony*, from a musical perspective, evokes the combination of chords that produce a pleasing effect, like "four-part harmony." It's also what is produced in a relationship when you have the combination of skills, attitudes, and attributes that work to produce a pleasing effect. And truth be told, you can have harmony on some relationship issues while other issues strike a grating and sometimes-harsh tone.

Here's what we suggest:

- Review the list of issues on page 10 of your Deep Love Report to see where the two of you are enjoying the most harmony. Focus for a moment on the top three items. Read them aloud and take time to consider each one and how they play out successfully in your relationship.

- Move to the next few items, those that make up the bulk of the middle of the list. Again read them aloud, taking your time to consider what they look like in your relationship. No need to discuss them just yet. Let them sink in as you both ponder the issues.

- Now look to the bottom three items on your list. Once more, read them aloud. Refrain from making any comments immediately.

Instead, think about what they mean and even what it would do for your relationship if you were more in tune with them together.

- Finally, review the list as a whole and note any issues where one of you is relatively content but the other is not.

Explore your customized list of the issues that are vital to any romantic relationship. Consider these questions:

- What do you think about your top three issues? Are they hard-won, or did they come easily?

- When you look at the middle items on your list, which ones have the two of you worked hardest on to find harmony? Which one would you celebrate most as a result of your intentional work together?

- What makes the bottom three items feel so out of tune in your attempts to create harmony together? Looking at it from the other side, what would it do for your relationship, in specific terms, if you were more in tune on these items?

Out of discord comes the fairest harmony.

Heraclitus of Ephesus

- On a scale of 1 to 10, how much intention has each of these bottom three items received from you in the past month or so?

- If you could press a magic button to instantly improve one of these bottom three items, which one would it be for you and why?

- Discuss any items where one of you is content and the other is not. What's going on? Be patient and sensitive to each other as you discuss these items.

- What can you do now? What kind of practical steps can you take? Can you both agree to focus specifically on one item from your list where you are both motivated to improve? Can you read a book together on the topic? Attend a seminar? Seek counsel? What do you plan to do together?

- Finally, go back to your future time line that you just created. How will working on the issues highlighted on page 10 make a difference in getting to where you want to be in the years ahead?

You may want to jot a note or two on the insights you now have as a result of your discussion:

_____

_____

_____

THE BOTTOM LINE

The greatest insight I got from this session is . . .

HIS	HERS
_____	_____
_____	_____
_____	_____
_____	_____

The one thing I'd like to do differently in our relationship as a result of this session is . . .

HIS	HERS
_____	_____
_____	_____
_____	_____
_____	_____

SESSION TAKEAWAY

You've invested in the Deep Love experience because you want the very best for your relationship. You want as much harmony as possible. You know that every couple has their issues, and these issues require work. The more intention you devote to creating harmony where you're experiencing discord, the deeper your love will grow. Your decisions create your destination as a couple.

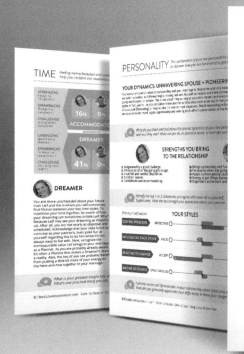

Report for:

BRIE & LEIF JENSEN
Married: 7/13/2005   Date Completed: 8/17/2016

DeepLoveAssessment.com

Take the Deep Love Assessment for just **$35 per couple** at Outreach.DeepLoveAssessment.com, and receive a FREE download, "10 Secrets to Hot Monogamy."

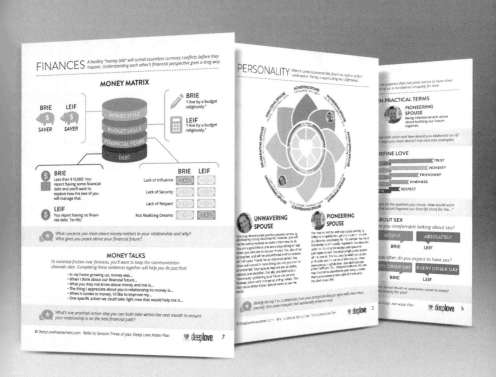

You won't find a more personalized and powerful relationship assessment than DEEP LOVE.

Each of the four sections of the report is essential to deepening the relationship with lasting, positive results:

1. **Personality**—because it's the best way to enhance empathy
2. **Communication**—because it's the lifeblood of love
3. **Conflict**—because every couple has friction
4. **Adaptability**—because even good relationships bump into bad things

ABOUT THE AUTHORS

Drs. Les and Leslie Parrott, psychologists and marriage and family therapists, are #1 *New York Times* best-selling authors and creators of the most widely used premarriage program in the world—*Saving Your Marriage Before It Starts*—trusted by more than a million couples and translated into more than twenty languages. Their renowned SYMBIS Assessment has been called a "game changer." *Love Talk*, *Your Time-Starved Marriage*, and *Crazy Good Sex* are among their landmark best sellers. Each year they speak live to more than fifty thousand people and have been featured on *Oprah*, *CBS This Morning*, *TODAY*, CNN, *The View*, and in *USA Today* and the *New York Times*. Les and Leslie live in Seattle, Washington, with their two sons. Learn more at **LesandLeslie.com**.